SNOW LEOPARD VS. WILD YAK

BY KIERAN DOWNS

BELLWETHER MEDIA • MINNEAPOLIS, MN

Torque brims with excitement
perfect for thrill-seekers of all kinds.
Discover daring survival skills, explore
uncharted worlds, and marvel at mighty
engines and extreme sports. In *Torque* books,
anything can happen. Are you ready?

This edition first published in 2022 by Bellwether Media, Inc.

No part of this publication may be reproduced in whole or in part without written
permission of the publisher. For information regarding permission, write to
Bellwether Media, Inc., Attention: Permissions Department,
6012 Blue Circle Drive, Minnetonka, MN 55343.

Library of Congress Cataloging-in-Publication Data

LC record for Snow Leopard vs. Wild Yak available
at https://lccn.loc.gov/2021039732

Editor: Rebecca Sabelko   Designer: Josh Brink

Printed in the United States of America, North Mankato, MN.

TABLE OF CONTENTS

THE COMPETITORS

Few animals can survive the harsh, cold mountains of Central Asia. Snow leopards **thrive** as one of the top **predators** of these mountains. They silently creep across the snow-covered slopes.

Wild yaks are also built for this **climate**. They can survive temperatures as low as -40 degrees Fahrenheit (-40 degrees Celsius)! Could they stand up to snow leopards?

SNOW LEOPARD PROFILE

LENGTH
**UP TO 5 FEET
(1.5 METERS)**

WEIGHT
**165 POUNDS
(75 KILOGRAMS)**

0   2 FEET   4 FEET   6 FEET

HABITAT

MOUNTAINS

SNOW LEOPARD RANGE

■ RANGE

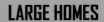

LARGE HOMES

Prey can be hard to find in the mountains, so snow leopards spread out. Their territories can be as large as 80 square miles (207 square kilometers)!

ROSETTES

Snow leopards live high in the mountain ranges of Central Asia. They have gray or tan fur spotted with dark **rosettes**. This helps them blend in with their surroundings.

Snow leopards normally live alone. They roam large **territories**. They mark their territories so other leopards stay away. Their main **prey** includes wild sheep, deer, and other **mammals**.

Wild yaks are large mammals. Their long fur is black or dark brown. They eat mosses and grasses found at high **elevations**.

Wild yaks live in herds on the Tibetan **Plateau**. They are the largest **native** animal found there. They can weigh more than 2,000 pounds (907 kilograms) and reach up to 11 feet (3.4 meters) long!

HIGH UP

Wild yaks can survive at elevations as high as 20,000 feet (6,096 meters)!

WILD YAK PROFILE

LENGTH
UP TO 11 FEET
(3.4 METERS)

WEIGHT
MORE THAN 2,000 POUNDS
(907 KILOGRAMS)

0   4 FEET   8 FEET   12 FEET

HABITAT

GRASSLANDS   ALPINE TUNDRA   MOUNTAINS

WILD YAK RANGE

☐ RANGE

SECRET WEAPONS

Snow leopards have wide, furry paws. The paws allow leopards to sneak around the mountains. Each paw has sharp claws used to grab prey.

Wild yaks have wide, hard hooves. These help yaks walk on snow and ice. The hooves also have thin, sharp tips that help yaks escape predators up steep slopes.

SNOW LEOPARD LEAPING DISTANCE

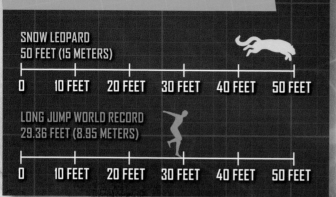

SNOW LEOPARD
50 FEET (15 METERS)

0	10 FEET	20 FEET	30 FEET	40 FEET	50 FEET

LONG JUMP WORLD RECORD
29.36 FEET (8.95 METERS)

0	10 FEET	20 FEET	30 FEET	40 FEET	50 FEET

Snow leopards have powerful back legs. These allow the cats to leap as far as 50 feet (15 meters)! Snow leopards easily jump across cliffs as they track prey. They pounce to make a kill.

SIZE CHART

WILD YAK HORNS
ABOUT 30 INCHES (76 CENTIMETERS)

Wild yaks have sharp horns on their heads. Their horns are mostly used to dig through snow and ice to find food. They also help fight off predators.

SECRET WEAPONS

WIDE PAWS

POWERFUL LEGS

LONG TAILS

Snow leopards follow prey through tough **terrain**. Long, thick tails keep them balanced on uneven ground. Their tails can be more than half the length of their bodies!

WILD YAK

WIDE HOOVES   SHARP HORNS   LARGE HERDS

Wild yaks travel in large herds. Some herds include as many as 200 yaks. The large groups keep yaks safe by scaring predators away.

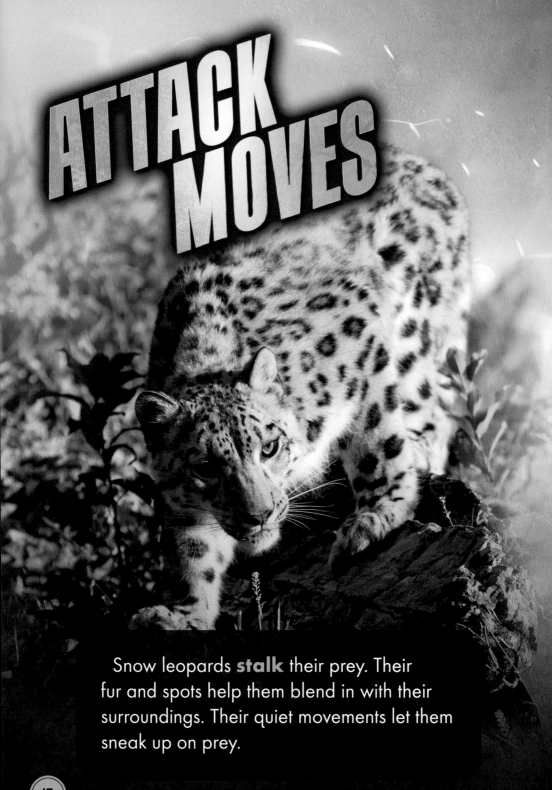

ATTACK MOVES

Snow leopards **stalk** their prey. Their fur and spots help them blend in with their surroundings. Their quiet movements let them sneak up on prey.

Wild yaks snort loudly when enemies approach. This often drives predators away. If this does not work, yaks may run. Sometimes, they charge!

A LONG HUNT

Snow leopards may track their prey for up to a week!

When the time is right, snow leopards **ambush** their prey. They jump onto the animal's back. They dig their claws into their prey's **flesh** while delivering deadly bites.

Wild yaks use herds for protection. Herds will form circles around young or sick members. They lower their horns so predators cannot get through.

READY, FIGHT!

A snow leopard tracks a lone yak. The leopard sneaks up on its prey. But the yak spots the leopard. It snorts to try to scare the leopard away.

But the hungry leopard is ready to fight. As the yak starts to run, the leopard leaps onto the yak's back. Its bites bring the yak down. The snow leopard has its meal!

GLOSSARY

ambush—to carry out a surprise attack

climate—the long-term weather conditions for certain areas

elevations—heights

flesh—the soft parts of an animal's body

mammals—warm-blooded animals that have backbones and feed their young milk

native—originally from the area

plateau—an area of flat, raised land

predators—animals that hunt other animals for food

prey—animals that are hunted by other animals for food

rosettes—the spots on a snow leopard

stalk—to follow closely and quietly

terrain—types of land

territories—home areas

thrive—to live well

TO LEARN MORE

AT THE LIBRARY

Adamson, Thomas K. *Anaconda vs. Jaguar*. Minneapolis, Minn.: Bellwether Media, 2020.

Bodden, Valerie. *Snow Leopards*. Mankato, Minn.: Creative Education, 2018.

Duling, Kaitlyn. *Wild Yaks*. Minneapolis, Minn.: Bellwether Media, 2021.

ON THE WEB

FACTSURFER

Factsurfer.com gives you a safe, fun way to find more information.

1. Go to www.factsurfer.com

2. Enter "snow leopard vs. wild yak" into the search box and click 🔍.

3. Select your book cover to see a list of related content.

INDEX